Credit goes to
the team of designers,
photographers, cartoonists,
and editor Dean Goodluck
at the publisher: D'Moon

Copyright ©D'Moon
third edition, second print: 2021
ebook edition: 2017
all rights reserved
except for reader comments and
poems & quotes not by LuCxeed

ISBN: 978-1-933187-98-3

Slight variations may occur
as part of the print-on-demand process
since each book is manufactured in its entirety.

Your feedback is most welcome ~
publisher@worldculturepictorial.com

Introduction

A ten-year journey
of Reading and Reflection,
sparkling with
knowledge and wisdom,
humour and diligence.

To thank the ever-appreciated
blessings, here comes
Three Steps Wiser,
leaping from on-line to off-line,
into fine-art quality press.
Enjoyable everywhere.

Each entry is a glimpse
as an invisible window
to a heart-touching story
(lost baby whale adopted yacht
as mom), amazing news or
character, or technology's
surprising advancement,
goings-on anywhere
geographically (British Queen
bought the largest wind
turbine while US was
enthusiastically engaged in
Iraq War);

in the time space, what happened in Year 366 is still on-going, fascinating! Each entry offers a link to relevant, stunning photos or further online exploration.

Layer by layer, no spoilers.

Gentle hearts moved, touching comments jotted. Millions of readers have dropped by, thousands have written messages (some of which come along in print) to share feelings and knowledge (conversation on CT scan spans years) or simply tell they've been here and enjoyed the read.

Wonderful experience and learning - regardless the happenings are awesome or absurd. Readers' thoughtful comments are truly encouraging and half-way testimonials to bring these books to more people as the famed do many other books.

Another uniqueness of Three Steps Wiser is to bring classic poems into modern life. Poetry lives beyond literature, and poets are beyond masters of languages. Classic poems also tell stories (The Sailor-Boy by John Clare). Poets lived their lives just as we do. The pain of losing a dear friend bleeds off the page in Samuel Taylor Coleridge's A Broken Friendship -
 "To free the hollow heart
    from painting -
 They stood aloof,
    the scars remaining".
Romance frequently visits and so does the shift of emotion. The confession in The Beginning (Rupert Brooke) reads:
 "And I loved you
    before you were old and wise,
 When the flame of youth
    was strong in your eyes,
 —And my heart is sick
    with memories."
Lovely to speak openly, or unforgivable for the change of heart? You can agree or disagree secretly.

We are created with vision
without limitation unless
limited by opportunities
to learn less.

Each volume offers around
100 invisible windows waiting
for you to open – enjoy the
fresh air, true stories from far
beyond horizon and time zone.
"This life is most jolly"!
(Shakespeare)

Knowledge instills confidence
to be prudent.
Wonderful.
Three steps wiser.

*World Culture Pictorial®

Publisher's Note

Nature seeds Earth with life and treasure. Could Man create Nature (with means of money and labs)? Some folks believe so and some not. Shakespeare's "Winter's Tale" seems refreshing as ever -

"PERDITA
For I have heard it said
There is an art which in their piedness shares
With great creating nature.

POLIXENES
Say there be;
Yet nature is made better by no mean
But nature makes that mean: so, over that art
Which you say adds to nature, is an art
That nature makes. You see, sweet maid, we marry
A gentler scion to the wildest stock,
And make conceive a bark of baser kind
By bud of nobler race: this is an art
Which does mend nature, change it rather, but
The art itself is nature."

Logic and keen observation.
Enlightened steps (though gravitated down to Earth, not up in the clouds) will sing!

Dean Goodluck

Contents

Beginning
Copyright
Title Page
Introduction
Publisher's Note
Table of Contents

Section 1

2008/08/10
"Look into the mirror of history
to see the history of tomorrow."
- LuCxeed

2008/08/10
All 3 superpowers
are super busy:
US, Russia, China

Three Steps Wiser - WcP Reading & Reflection Vol. 03

Contents

2008/08/11
"The hidden harmony
is better than the obvious."
- Heraclitus

2008/08/11
Impact of Iraq War:
expected or unexpected?

2008/08/12
A giant Royal Caribbean
cruise ship, a floating city

2008/08/12
"There is one order of beauty..."
- George Eliot

2008/08/13
It's one of the largest. It can fly
only a few meters above water

Dean Goodluck

Contents

2008/08/14
FIVE dogs identical to dead one
wake you up at night?!

2008/08/16
Sooner than estimated:
minorities will be majority

2008/08/17
Disney characters,
famous yet behind bars

2008/08/18
Baby humpback, lost,
bonds with yacht

2008/08/20
1594. Amsterdam.
Dutch merchants founded
"Company of Far Lands"

Three Steps Wiser - WtP Reading & Reflection Vol. 03

Contents

2008/08/21
Greenland,
a land of sparkling ice and snow

2008/08/22
Planet Earth choking.
Each year 500 billion to
1 trillion more plastic bags

2008/08/23
Phone rings:
3am ET on Saturday

2008/08/24
2008 Olympics. 200 countries'
5,000 hours of coverage,
842 million (twice US
population) locals viewed

Dean Goodluck

Contents

2008/08/25
25 Aug 1609.
Galilei Galileo demonstrates
his first telescope

2008/08/26
Humor rewarded

2008/08/27
Iraq demands
all foreign troops out of sight

2008/08/28
Dream job, dreamed
vocation vacations

2008/08/29
ONE day. Brad Pitt becomes hero,
rescues young fan, and
picks up Best Actor trophy

Three Steps Wiser - WcP Reading & Reflection Vol. 03

Contents

2008/08/30
Cosmic smash-up:
energetic collision between
two large galaxy clusters

2008/08/31
Farming goes vertical,
up into sky

2008/09/01
Only panda born in US
so far

2008/09/02
Browser wars:
Google's Chrome
takes on Microsoft

Dean Goodluck

Contents

2008/09/03
"I leave you free from both men"
- Saint's last words in Year 366

2008/09/04
Dr. Ron Paul,
candidate in 2008 election,
once called "Young Lion" and
"Lion of Liberty", never yields

2008/09/05
The largest vessel ever sunk
to make a reef:
44,000 tons, 888-foot long

2008/09/05
Chunk of ice shelf
size of Manhattan
breaks away from Arctic

Three Steps Wiser - WcP Reading & Reflection Vol. 03

Contents

2008/09/06
Electric minivan?
Sounds attractive

2008/09/07
Norwegian Sir with wings:
knighted penguin
Sir Nils Olav

2008/09/07
"A woman knows
the face of the man she loves
like a sailor knows the open sea."
- Honoré de Balzac

2008/09/08
Fallen for WALL-E?
More animation films
reconnect with Nature

Dean Goodluck

Contents

2008/09/09
Roger Federer now just
one win away from breaking
Pete Sampras' record of
14 Grand Slam titles

2008/09/10
It's physics.
Biggest and most complex
machine on Earth,
Large Hadron Collider
fires first beam

2008/09/11
"There was never a good war
or a bad peace."
– Benjamin Franklin

2008/09/12
Fashion in a slimmer economy

Three Steps Wiser - WeP Reading & Reflection Vol. 03

Contents

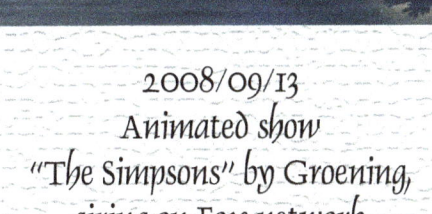

2008/09/13
Animated show
"The Simpsons" by Groening,
airing on Fox network,
longest-running comedy
in prime time

2008/09/14
"Perfect Flight":
Air New Zealand
cuts waiting time,
trims flying time,
saves 1,200 gallons of fuel

2008/09/15
Collective poetry book:
a solid year 1797-1798,
Wordsworth and Coleridge
had nothing but inspiration

Dean Goodluck

Contents

2008/09/16
Downward spiral:
158-year-old Lehman Brothers
filed largest bankruptcy;
Merrill Lynch sold

2008/09/17
"History is a race between
education and catastrophe."
- H. G. Wells

2008/09/18
Time for zero-emission car:
all-electric luxury Tesla sedan
on the way

2008/09/19
"Do I really want that CT scan?"
A chest CT scan is equivalent to
about 100 X-rays

Three Steps Wiser - WeP Reading & Reflection Vol. 03

Contents

2008/09/20
Southern Hemisphere Paris?
"Foodie" often heard
in Melbourne

2008/09/21
"Romance like a ghost escapes
touching; it is always where
you are not, not where you are..."
- George William Curtis

2008/09/22
Tony Blair's point of view
at Yale

2008/09/23
Large Hadron Collider,
the most powerful atom smasher,
switched on two weeks ago,
now hibernates

Dean Goodluck

Contents

2008/09/24
"Earth provides enough to satisfy
every man's need,
but not every man's greed."
- Mahatma Gandhi

2008/09/25
Stock market's wild swings -
rich gets richer,
and someone gets poorer

2008/09/26
First spacewalk:
three decades of hoping,
ten years of training

2008/09/27
Fusionman
"flies a little bit like a bird" with
homemade rocket-powered wing

Three Steps Wiser - WeP Reading & Reflection Vol. 03

Contents

2008/09/28
Paul Newman,
a consummate charmer,
dedicated himself to
his cause, racing cars,
wife and family

2008/09/29
3 technology powers
US, Russia, now China,
have their astronauts
walk in space

2008/09/30
Hometown.
They sing, rehearse, perform,
and they are in their eighties

Dean Goodluck

Contents

2008/09/30
Poem
"Freeze, freeze thou bitter sky,
That does not bite so nigh
As benefits forgot"
- William Shakespeare

2008/10/01
3rd most popular
in the race
in most opinion polls: 2008

2008/10/02
Math.
$700 billion to bail out
drained $635 billion

2008/10/03
Queen Elizabeth II's vision to
reign over the wind

Three Steps Wiser - W&P Reading & Reflection Vol. 03

Contents

2008/10/04
EV show in Paris.
Two years ago,
electric cars impossible

2008/10/05
Brazilian coastguards'
air force plane offers
lost young penguins
a free ride

2008/10/06
Poem in Art
"So fled thy soul into the realms
above, / Regions of peace and
everlasting love"
- John Keats

Dean Goodluck

Contents

2008/10/06
Luckiest photographer
met Einstein, Churchill,
Picasso, and Hemingway

2008/10/07
5,487 mammals on Earth:
76 gone, 1,141 in danger of
extinction

2008/10/08
How big is 10 trillion? Its digits
beat National Debt Clock
in New York

2008/10/09
1783, birth of hot air balloons
carrying human passengers

Three Steps Wiser - WeP Reading & Reflection Vol. 03

Contents

2008/10/10
"It is a thousand times better to
have common sense without
education than to have education
without common sense."
- Robert Green Ingersoll

2008/10/11
Night is not what it was
- how do you feel with
light everywhere?

2008/10/12
1492. Columbus' journal:
"as I saw that they (local natives)
were very friendly to us"

2008/10/12
Aristophanes: "Shall I crack
any of those old jokes, master...?"

Dean Goodluck

Contents

Section 2

"Wine is bottled poetry."
- Robert Louis Stevenson
Let's toast
~ Leisure reading
along the journey of
publishing this book

Poem in Art
Ode To Napoleon Buonaparte
- Lord Byron
"'Tis done--but yesterday a King!
And arm'd with Kings to strive--
And now thou art a nameless thing...
To those that worshipp'd thee;
Nor till thy fall could mortals guess
Ambition's less than littleness!"

Three Steps Wiser - WcP Reading & Reflection Vol. 03

Contents

Poem
A Broken Friendship
- Samuel Taylor Coleridge
"Alas! they had been friends in youth;
But whispering tongues
can poison truth"

Poem in Art
"Nature" Is What We See
- Emily Dickinson

Poem in Art
The Beginning
- Rupert Brooke
"Some day I shall rise
and leave my friends
And seek you again
through the world's far ends,
You whom I found so fair"

Dean Goodluck

Contents

Poem
The Sailor-Boy
- John Clare
"'Tis three years and a quarter
since I left my own fireside
To go aboard a ship through love,
and plough the ocean wide."

Poem
Paradise Lost: Book 01
(lines 392-543)
- John Milton

Poem in Art
A Character
- William Wordsworth
"I marvel how Nature
could ever find space
For so many strange contrasts
in one human face"

Three Steps Wiser - WcP Reading & Reflection Vol. 03
Contents

❅❅❅

World Culture Pictorial®
WcP Blog
Book Covers of Other Volumes
in this Series

Dean Goodluck

2008/08/10
WCP.Philosophy

Look into the mirror of history to see the history of tomorrow.

"Look into
the mirror of history
to see
the history of tomorrow."
- LuCxeed

www.worldculturepictorial.com/blog/archive/all/2008/08/10

Three Steps Wiser - WcP Reading & Reflection Vol. 03

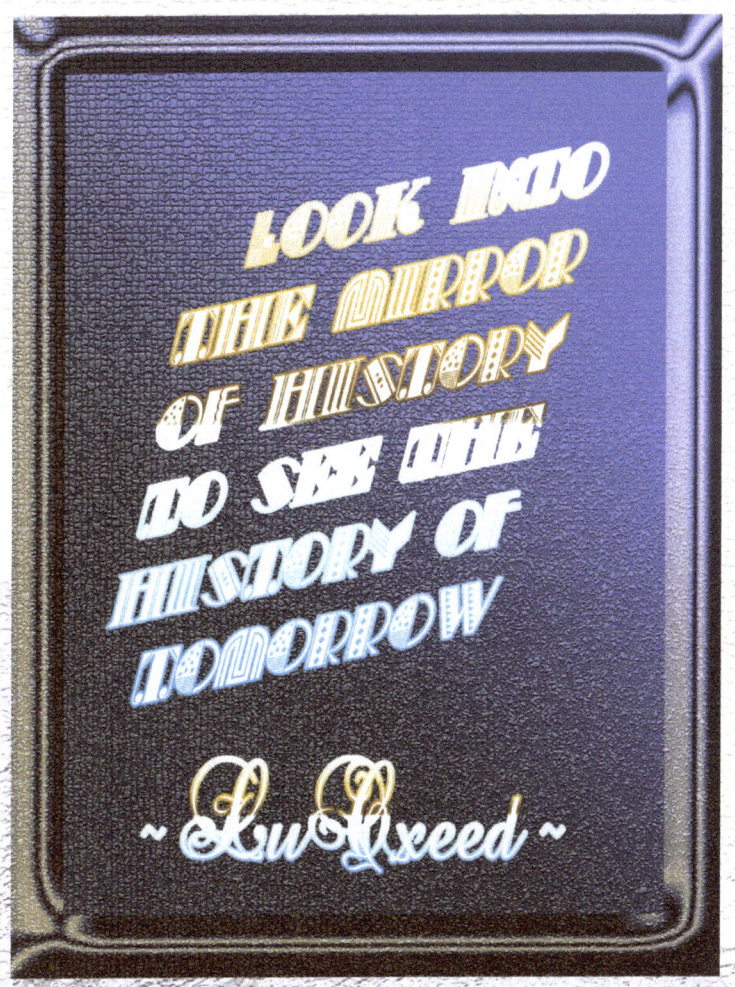

LOOK INTO THE MIRROR OF HISTORY TO SEE THE HISTORY OF TOMORROW

~ LuPxeed ~

Dean Goodluck

2008/08/10
WcP.Tomorrows.History

All 3 superpowers are super busy:
US, Russia, China

US tied up in Iraq.
China focused on Olympics.
Russian tanks and troops into Ossetia, part of former Soviet republic of Georgia

www.worldculturepictorial.com/blog/archive/all/2008/08/10

Three Steps Wiser - WcP Reading & Reflection Vol. 03

2008/08/11
WcP.Philosophy

The hidden harmony is better than the obvious.

"The hidden harmony is better than the obvious."
- Heraclitus

www.worldculturepictorial.com/blog/archive/all/2008/08/11

Dean Goodluck

2008/08/11
WcP.Tomorrows.History

Impact of Iraq War: expected or unexpected?

Impact of Iraq War: US weakened. EU distracted. Russia's $18.9 bil trade surplus and troops deeper into Georgia - nations panic

www.worldculturepictorial.com/blog/archive/all/2008/08/11

Three Steps Wiser - WcP Reading & Reflection Vol. 03

2008/08/12
WcP.Scientific.Mind

A giant Royal Caribbean cruise ship, a floating city

At sea, the bigger, the better? "Oasis of the Sea", largest cruise ship, tall as a 12-story building, wider than Panama Canal

www.worldculturepictorial.com/blog/archive/all/2008/08/12

Dean Goodluck

2008/08/12
WcP.Art

There is one order of beauty...

"There is one order of beauty
which seems made to turn heads.
It is a beauty like that of kittens,
or very small downy ducks making gentle
rippling noises with their soft bills,
or babies just beginning to toddle."
- George Eliot

www.worldculturepictorial.com/blog/archive/all/2008/08/12

Three Steps Wiser - WcP Reading & Reflection Vol. 03

2008/08/13
WcP.Scientific.Mind

*It's one of the largest.
It can fly only a few
meters above water*

Missions of the largest aircrafts: Western H-4 Hercules and Airbus A380, Russia's Antonov An-225 Mriya and "Caspian Sea Monster"

www.worldculturepictorial.com/blog/archive/all/2008/08/13

Reader Comments

(not in chronological order)
- 2016/07/08 - "This article about the missions of the largest aircraft is found to be very informative. I have learned new factors about the aircraft and related things. Hope the blog will share more interesting things like this and thank you so much for providing such valuable info."

- 2016/11/20 - "Thanks for sharing with a fan of aerial news."
- 2010/11/20 - "Antonov is from Ukraine, not Russia."
- 2012/01/12 - "Yes it is manufactured in Ukraine Factory Soviet union time but if you will search the Antonov which build this aircraft is from Russia..."
- 2016/04/06 - "Thank you for sharing this post here!!!!"
- 2010/11/20 - "And "Mriya" (dream) - ukrainian word. Russian - "Mechta"."
- 2016/04/03 - "I am an anthropology student and this site has helped me a lot to know more about the various cultures across the world. This is the reason I visit the site so often. Keep on sharing more and more posts like this. Thank you."

Three Steps Wiser - WcP Reading & Reflection Vol. 03

2008/08/14
WcP.Common.Sense

FIVE dogs identical to dead one wake you up at night?!

All the same: clone breaching life's uniqueness? South Korea reveals 1st dog clones - 1 dead dog into 5 identical ones

www.worldculturepictorial.com/blog/archive/all/2008/08/14

Dean Goodluck

2008/08/16
WCP.Watchful.Eye

Sooner than estimated: minorities will be majority

8 years sooner than previously estimated: US minorities will be the majority by 2042

www.worldculturepictorial.com/blog/archive/all/2008/08/16

Three Steps Wiser - WcP Reading & Reflection Vol. 03

2008/08/17
WcP.Story.Teller

Disney characters, famous yet behind bars

Mickey and Goofy behind bars? Snow White, Tinkerbell, Peter Pan handcuffed

www.worldculturepictorial.com/blog/archive/all/2008/08/17

Reader Comments

♦ 2016/04/27 - "Nice read, I just passed this onto a colleague who was doing some research on that. And he actually bought me lunch as I found it for him (smile). Therefore let me rephrase that: Thanks for lunch!"

♦ 2016/04/27 - "What's taking place, I'm new to this, I stumbled upon this, I've found it positively helpful and it has helped me out loads. I hope to give contribution and aid different customers like it's helped me. Good job."

Dean Goodluck

2008/08/18
WcP.Story.Teller

Baby humpback, lost, bonds with yacht

Lone baby humpback whale lost in Sydney waters, 'adopts' yacht as mom

www.worldculturepictorial.com/blog/archive/all/2008/08/18

(not in chronological order)
- 2016/04/25 - "Poor little whale, but it's so cute. The way he adopt the yatch as his mom :3"
- 2015/10/05 - "Such a heart touching story. Poor whale."
- 2015/09/28 - "This is very very bad news. Poor whale. Sydney government should find the whale and take him back to safety."

Three Steps Wiser - WcP Reading & Reflection Vol. 03

- 2015/10/05 - "I liked your article and I hope you will have many entries or more."
- 2015/07/27 - "Poor whale...I hope it's fine now."
- 2016/10/12 - "I must appreciate the way you have expressed your feelings through your blog!"
- 2015/03/31 - "I feel sad for the whale. I don't know whether killing it was a good idea. They should just probably let it go by itself and let fate decides what would happen to it. Anyway, Thanks for sharing!"
- 2014/07/15 - "This is certainly one of the most interesting and amusing news I have read recently. I wonder how such a big fish goes missing from its mother's cradle. I followed the news link and came to know that they had to drop the baby for its own survival."
- 2016/01/20 - "Sad to hear that. This is such heart touching news. I am very much disappointed."
- 2015/04/27 - "Poor baby whale!"
- 2015/11/04 - "I wanted to thank you for this interesting post. I definitely loved every little bit of it."
- 2015/03/14 - "Love this post."
- 2015/04/21 - "The calf comes into view beat but savors hope it will persist out to sea and look for its mother or any more pod of whales."

- 2016/05/12 - "I found lots of interesting information here. Great work. Thanks for the share, loved reading the article, please do share more like this with us."
- 2008/08/21 - "Lure it to a pod. Or does it make too cute and sad a story?"
- 2015/03/02 - "Oh, it's a whale. They seem to be very dangerous. But is it really so?"
- 2016/04/15 - "You have a real ability for writing unique content. I like how you think and the way you represent your views in this article. I agree with your way of thinking. Thank you for sharing."
- 2016/04/19 - "I would very much like to agree with the previous commenter! I find this blog really useful for my uni project. I hope to add more useful posts later."
- 2016/11/29 - "Thank your site! Information you share is useful to me! it's great that I know this site."
- 2015/01/29 - "Amid the winter, humpbacks live off their fat stores. Their eating methodology comprises generally of krill and little fish. Humpbacks have a differing collection of sustaining systems, including the air pocket net encouraging method."

Three Steps Wiser - WcP Reading & Reflection Vol. 03

- 2016/08/01 - "You've written nice post, I am gonna bookmark this page, thanks for info. I actually appreciate your own position and I will be sure to come back here."
- 2016/04/15 - "Thanks, you guys that is a great explanation. keep up the good work in your granite blog."
- 2016/01/08 - "Wonderful blog! This is very informative site. I am totally pleased by your excellent work. Many thanks for sharing."
- 2016/07/18 - "Good job. All of them are useful!"
- 2016/11/17 - "Many thanks for sharing the information in your blog."
- 2016/04/06 - "Excellent post! I read your article and i think this is really too enjoyable."
- 2014/09/18 - "The post is written in satisfyingly and honest manner and I gathered valuable details from this superb post."
- 2016/02/03 - "This article is such great reading material and timely effort seems on it. Keep sharing here!"
- 2016/01/27 - "I am really taking interest by reading fundamental points. Keeping posting like this!"
- 2015/10/15 - "I am very happy to discover your post as it will become top in my collection of favorite blogs to visit."

- 2015/06/05 - "Great! Thanks for sharing the information. That is very helpful for increasing my knowledge in this field."
- 2015/01/22 - "It is telling about lone baby humpback lost in Sydney waters."
- 2016/05/22 - "Two things are infinite: the universe and human stupidity. And I'm not sure about the universe."
- 2016/05/22 - "There are only two ways to live your life. One is as though nothing is a miracle. The other is as though everything is a miracle."
- 2016/08/07 - "Nice words."
- 2014/09/27 - "This is so informative and all the time current topic. The specified elements touch on the accurate points."
- 2015/07/14 - "I agree with your comment. I think this is very useful info! Thanks!"
- 2014/10/04 - "Consistent content creation! Your topic is comprehensive to gain excellent info and much exposure. Keep writing!"
- 2015/07/02 - "This is a great web site. Good sparkling user interface and very informative blogs. I'll be coming back in a bit, thanks for the great article. I've found it enormously useful..."

Three Steps Wiser - WcP Reading & Reflection Vol. 03

2008/08/20
WcP.Tomorrows.History

1594. Amsterdam. Dutch merchants founded "Company of Far Lands"

20 Aug 1597. Dutch East India Company's first fleet of four ships returns to The Netherlands from the Far East

www.worldculturepictorial.com/ blog/ archive/ all/ 2008/ 08/ 20

Dean Goodluck

2008/08/21
WCP.Scientific.Mind

Greenland, a land of sparkling ice and snow

Amazing photos from Greenland, where unfortunately ice runs away by hundreds of billions of tons a year

www.worldculturepictorial.com/blog/archive/all/2008/08/21

Reader Comments

- 2011/05/12 - "Very cool pictures - thanks for sharing them!"
- 2017/01/16 - "beautiful ice pictures"
- 2017/01/21 - "Wow amazing photography it was. These pictures have revealed many things to me as I can know how the scientists are working hard for research there. But I am confused what are they trying to find in icebergs."

Three Steps Wiser - WcP Reading & Reflection Vol. 03

2008/08/22
WcP.life.Coach

*Planet Earth choking.
Each year 500 billion to
1 trillion more plastic bags*

Our planet would be less burdened if everyone can use 10 fewer bags per month, reuse 10 plastic beverage bottles

www.worldculturepictorial.com/blog/archive/all/2008/08/22

Dean Goodluck

2008/08/23
WcP.Observer

Phone rings:
3am ET on Saturday

3 a.m. call. Obama announces running mate: Joe Biden, six-term senator from Delaware

www.worldculturepictorial.com/blog/archive/all/2008/08/23

Three Steps Wiser - WcP Reading & Reflection Vol. 03

2008/08/24
WcP.Story.Teller

*2008 Olympics. 200 countries'
5,000 hours of coverage,
842 million (twice US population)
locals viewed*

Parties of the century: closing ceremony as well as opening ceremony of 2008 Beijing Olympic Games

www.worldculturepictorial.com/ blog/ archive/ all/ 2008/ 08/ 24

Dean Goodluck

2008/08/25
WCP.Scientific.Mind

25 Aug 1609. Galileo Galilei demonstrates his first telescope

Galileo, called Father of Modern Science by Einstein, was born into a musical family in Pisa

www.worldculturepictorial.com/blog/archive/all/2008/08/25

Three Steps Wiser - WcP Reading & Reflection Vol. 03

2008/08/26
WcP.Humor

Humor rewarded

Three writers finalists for American humor award - the Thurber Prize: Larry Doyle, Patricia Marx, and Simon Rich

www.worldculturepictorial.com/ blog/ archive/ all/ 2008/ 08/ 26

Dean Goodluck

2008/08/27
WcP.Observer

Iraq demands all foreign troops out of sight

Iraq Prime Minister pushes for firm withdrawal date, demands all foreign troops out by 2011

www.worldculturepictorial.com/blog/archive/all/2008/08/27

Three Steps Wiser - WcP Reading & Reflection Vol. 03

2008/08/28
WcP.Story.Teller

*Dream job,
dreamed vocation vacations*

What is your dream job? Among Vocation Vacations' top 20: actor, chocolatier, voice-over artist, wedding planner

www.worldculturepictorial.com/ blog/ archive/ all/ 2008/ 08/ 28

Reader Comments

♦ 2012/01/28 - "I've never dreamed a dog day-care owner could be a job someone dreams of. I guess I see the reason why somebody would want to do that though, because you get to go out for walks and get money from it. After taking pre-employment testing, I've decided I'm good to be a salesman. Not a job most of us dream of, but I always strive for something other than the usual."

Dean Goodluck

2008/08/29
WCP.Movie.Critic

ONE day. Brad Pitt becomes hero, rescues young fan, and picks up Best Actor trophy

Brad Pitt rescues soaking fan from lake at 65th annual Venice Film Festival, and picks up Best Actor trophy from 2007

www.worldculturepictorial.com/ blog/ archive/ all/ 2008/ 08/ 29

Three Steps Wiser - WcP Reading & Reflection Vol. 03

2008/08/30
WcP.Scientific.Mind

Cosmic smash-up:
energetic collision between
two large galaxy clusters

Galactic clash unmasks dark matter:
ordinary matter and dark matter separate
as two massive galaxies collide

www.worldculturepictorial.com/blog/archive/all/2008/08/30

Dean Goodluck

2008/08/31
WcP.System.Thinker

Farming goes vertical, up into sky

Towers of food, farms in the sky: self-sustaining skyscrapers in the city, vertical farming gains new interest

www.worldculturepictorial.com/blog/archive/all/2008/08/31

Three Steps Wiser - WcP Reading & Reflection Vol. 03

2008/09/01
WcP.Story.Teller

Only panda born in US so far

Zoo Atlanta celebrates arrival of baby panda, 2nd cub of mother Lun Lun and only panda born in US in 2008 so far

www.worldculturepictorial.com/blog/archive/all/2008/09/01

Reader Comments

(not in chronological order)
- 2016/12/02 - "So happy to see those cute little pandas with their mother panda. They have been facing extinction problems for a while now and it is pointed out in the post that this is the first panda born in US on 2008 so far. Thanks for sharing the post."
- 2016/08/24 - "Really really amazing... I love baby pandas... I'll be back to view your new post."

- 2015/06/27 – "I've never seen such amazing thoughts displayed in composing. Your author has an extremely one of a kind method for exhibiting data so as to catch the peruser's consideration."
- 2015/07/10 – "I will check your different articles without further ado. Continuously so fascinating to visit your site. Thank you for sharing, this will help me such a great amount in my learning."
- 2015/07/16 – "Your configuration, man… too astonishing! I can't hold up to peruse what you've got next. Thanks for your superb posting!"
- 2016/11/28 – "I am unquestionably making the most of your site. You unquestionably have some extraordinary knowledge and incredible stories."
- 2016/11/15 – "Excellent article. Very interesting to read. I really love to read such a nice article. Thanks! Keep rocking."
- 2016/01/21 – "So quiet panda, I like…"
- 2016/11/15 – "This is also a very good post which I really enjoyed reading. It is not every day that I have the possibility to see something like this."
- 2016/11/15 – "I am very happy to read this. This blog was really an awesome site which I had never found it anywhere, keep posting."

Three Steps Wiser - WcP Reading & Reflection Vol. 03

- 2016/11/25 - "This is my first time visit here and I found so much interesting stuff in your blog especially its discussion, thank you."
- 2016/03/05 - "I really enjoyed reading this article. I hope that other readers will also experience how I feel after reading your article. Thank you so much."
- 2016/12/08 - "You know your projects stand out of the herd. There's something special about them. It seems to me all of them are really brilliant!"
- 2016/01/05 - "Great Effort!! Loved it. Thanks for the post."
- 2016/02/17 - "Anyways I'm here now and could just like to say thanks for a tremendous post and an all round entertaining website. Please do keep up the great work."
- 2016/02/09 - "Hi there! Nice post! Please tell us when I will see a follow up!"
- 2015/10/18 - "Extremely intriguing. I truly love to peruse such a decent article. Much appreciated!"
- 2016/04/29 - "I always spend half an hour to read this website's articles daily along with a mug of coffee."
- 2016/12/08 - "I just got to this amazing site not long ago. I was actually captured with the resources you have got here. Big thumbs up for making such a wonderful blog page."

- 2016/11/28 - "This is a smart blog. I mean it. You have so much knowledge about this issue, and so much passion. You also know how to make people rally behind it, obviously from the responses."
- 2016/11/28 - "Really loved reading your blog. It was very well authored and easy to undertand. Unlike additional blogs I have read which are really not that good."
- 2016/01/29 - "I love the way you write and share your niche! Very interesting and different! Keep it coming!"
- 2016/12/12 - "I've been surfing online more than three hours today, yet I never found any interesting article like yours. It's pretty worth enough for me."
- 2015/07/08 - "Thank you for sharing, felt happy once reading in this blog, so much insight... hopefully always given the health and success always."
- 2016/12/12 - "Yes I totally agree with this article and I just want to say that this is a very nice and very informative article. I will make sure to be reading your blog more. You made a good point but I can't help but wonder, what about the other side? !!!!!!THANKS!!!!!!"
- 2016/12/10 - "Nice post! This is a very nice blog that I will definitively come back to more times this year! Thanks for informative post."

Three Steps Wiser - WcP Reading & Reflection Vol. 03

- 2016/12/10 - "I appreciate everything you have added to my knowledge base. Admiring the time and effort you put into your blog and detailed information you offer. Thanks."
- 2016/12/10 - "This is also a very good post which I really enjoyed reading. Thank you very much for this informative post."
- 2015/10/03 - "Thanks for this great post, I admire what you have done here."
- 2015/12/16 - "Awesome work! That is quite appreciated. I hope you'll get more success."
- 2016/12/10 - "I found so much entertaining stuff in your blog, especially its discussion. From the tons of comments on your articles, I guess I am not the only one having all the leisure here!"
- 2016/12/08 - "First You got a great blog. I will be interested in more similar topics. I see you got really very useful topics, I will be always checking your blog, thanks."
- 2016/12/08 - "It was a very good post indeed. I thoroughly enjoyed reading it in my lunch time. Will surely come and visit this blog more often. Thanks for sharing."
- 2016/12/04 - "Wishing you the best of luck for all your blogging efforts. This is my first-time visit here."

- 2015/06/25 - "Mind boggling posting! I really like the way you are sharing the exceptional subject."
- 2016/11/15 - "You have even managed to make it understandable and easy to read. You have some real writing talent. Thank you."
- 2016/11/14 - "Be sure to keep doing the terrific job that I will enjoy even more your impressive blog articles."
- 2016/11/14 - "Awesome blog. I enjoyed reading your articles. This is truly a great read for me. I have bookmarked it and I am looking forward to reading new articles. Keep up the good work!"
- 2016/11/15 - "A debt of gratitude is in order for setting aside an ideal opportunity to talk about this, I feel firmly about it and love adapting more on this subject."
- 2016/11/14 - "This post has helped me to have another perspective. I am researching this topic for a paper I am writing. Your article provided me great insight of my topic."
- 2016/11/13 - "I think this is one of the most significant information for me. And I'm glad reading your article. But should remark on some general things. The web site style is perfect. The articles are really great :D Good job. Cheers."

Three Steps Wiser - WcP Reading & Reflection Vol. 03

- 2016/11/13 - "...the world, and do anything I want to do. But as opposed to a citizen without a country, I actually feel today as a citizen of the world. And boy, am I finally enjoying this ride!"
- 2016/10/31 - "Thanks for taking the time to discuss this. I feel strongly about it and love learning more on this topic. If possible, as you gain expertise, would you mind updating your blog with more information? It is extremely helpful for me."
- 2016/11/02 - "Thanks for making such a cool post which is really very well written. Will be referring a lot of friends about this. Keep blogging."
- 2015/09/25 - "A good blog always comes up with new and exciting information and while reading I feel that this blog really has all the quality that qualifies a blog to be one. I wanted to leave a little comment to support you and wish you a good continuation. Wishing you the best of luck for all your blogging efforts."
- 2016/08/25 - "I was simply perusing along and happened upon your web journal. Simply needed to say great online journal and this article truly helped me."

- 2016/07/14 - "I Love to read your blog, Waiting for more updates and I already read your recent posts. Thanks for sharing this wonderful article with us."
- 2016/07/02 - "I recently found many useful information in your website especially this blog page. Among lots of comments on your articles. Thanks for sharing."
- 2016/06/27 - "Awesome article! I want people to know just how good this information is in your article. It's interesting, compelling content. Your views are much like my own concerning this subject."
- 2016/06/17 - "I think this is an informative post and it is very useful and knowledgeable. therefore, I would like to thank you for the efforts you have made in writing this article."
- 2016/05/20 - "Awesome article, it was exceptionally helpful! I simply began in this and I'm becoming more acquainted with it better! Cheers, keep doing awesome!"
- 2016/05/01 - "I got your blog yesterday and still I am waiting for the new posts... this is quite satisfying blog so all guys come here and learn something special."

Three Steps Wiser - WcP Reading & Reflection Vol. 03

- 2016/01/26 - "This blog is the book which I have feelings for around their lives. Will you produce intense addons."
- 2016/04/10 - "It is genuinely what I expected that would see trust in future you will continue in sharing such a stunning post."
- 2016/04/02 - "I like how you think and the way you relate to your perspectives in this article. I concur with your viewpoint. I truly loved looking at your web journal."
- 2016/03/26 - "Your style is unique compared to other folks I have read stuff from. I appreciate you for posting when you've got the opportunity, Guess I will just book mark this site."
- 2016/03/20 - "Amazingly beguiling to inspect this article. I may need to thank you for the endeavors you had made for making this splendid article."
- 2016/02/29 - "It's superior to anything normal to see that several individuals still see how to make a quality post!"
- 2016/02/24 - "You are sharing your uncommon online diary with us. An obligation of appreciation is all together to share and keep sharing."

- 2016/02/19 - "This kind of document is really good, along with my spouse and I get pleasure from all of the work that you have put into that. I think that you will be generating a truly interesting point. We had been additionally amazed. Very good function!"
- 2016/02/18 - "This is really unbelievable.. I am also finding this kind of post you have written very pretty. Thanks for sharing this kind of information."
- 2015/11/26 - "This post is truly glorious. I really like this post. It is one of the best posts that I've analyzed in quite a while."
- 2015/12/24 - "Thanks for a very interesting blog. What else may I get that kind of info written in such a perfect approach? I've a undertaking that I am simply now operating on, and I have been on the lookout for such info."
- 2016/02/21 - "Wonderfully created post, if perhaps just about all writers provided exactly the same degree of content material as you, the web will be a far better location. Make sure you continue the good work!"
- 2016/01/25 - "I have read your blog it is very helpful for me. I want to say thanks to you. I have bookmarked your site for future updates."

- 2015/11/18 - "Your site is incredibly distinctive from others. I am actually happy to view your own post. Thanks."
- 2015/10/25 - "I highly appreciate this post. It's hard to find the good from the bad sometimes, but I think you've nailed it! Would you mind updating your blog with more information?"
- 2015/10/10 - "I fit in with your conclusions and will eagerly look forward to your next updates. Just saying thanks will not just be sufficient, for the fantastic lucidity in your writing. I will instantly grab your RSS feed to stay informed of any updates."
- 2015/09/30 - "I delighted in perusing your articles. This is really an incredible read for me. I have bookmarked it and I am anticipating perusing new articles."
- 2015/09/28 - "Also, it's outstanding I have discovered your site. It's truly astonishing to peruse this sort of post."
- 2015/09/20 - "You make so many great points here that I read your article a couple of times. Your views are in accordance with my own for the most part. This is great content for your readers."
- 2016/01/24 - "Nice blog like this having great fun this blog amaze me..."

- 2015/09/23 - "This is an awesome motivating article. I am practically satisfied with your great work."
- 2016/02/21 - "Your content is nothing short of brilliant in many ways."
- 2015/09/11 - "This type of message is always inspiring and I prefer to read quality content, so happy to find good place to many here in the post, the writing is just great, thanks for the post."
- 2015/08/26 - "I can't stay without respecting your post it's truly magnificent a debt of gratitude is in order for sharing such decent substance."
- 2015/08/24 - "I'm eager to reveal this page. I have to thank you for one's time for this especially awesome read!!"
- 2015/08/19 - "Thanks for the nice blog. It was very useful for me. I'm happy I found this blog. Thank you for sharing with us, I too always learn something new from your post."
- 2015/07/18 - "I simply want to tell you that I am new to weblog and definitely liked this blog site. Very likely I'm going to bookmark your blog..."

- 2015/08/19 - "It was a wonderful chance to visit this kind of site and I am happy to know."
- 2015/08/23 - "Thanks for posting this info. I just want to let you know that I just checked out your site and I find it very interesting and informative. I can't wait to read lots of your posts."
- 2015/07/03 - "I prefer to study this kind of material. Nicely written information in this post, the quality of content is fine and the conclusion is lovely. Things are very open and intensely clear explanation of issues."
- 2015/06/27 - "I finally found great post here. I will get back here. I just added your blog to my bookmark sites. Thanks..."
- 2015/06/16 - "Thank you very much for such an interesting post, and I meet them more often when I visited this site..."
- 2015/06/15 - "Your online journal is so fascinating and exceptionally informative. Thanks for sharing."
- 2015/06/13 - "I unquestionably appreciated all of it and I have bookmarked your site to look at the new stuff you post in the future."

- 2015/06/06 - "This is a fantastic website and I can not recommend you guys enough. I really appreciate your post. It is very helpful for all the people on the web."
- 2014/10/25 - "Thanks for this great post, I find it very interesting and very well thought out and put together. I look forward to reading your work in the future."
- 2017/02/12 - "Thank for sharing! Great! Always so interesting to visit your site!"
- 2017/12/09 - "Very informative written post. The writer here has done a great job. I personally use them exclusively high-quality elements. I would love to see more of the same from you. Thank you for discussing this great post."
- 2014/11/10 - "I am very much overwhelmed by your thoughts for this particular story. A more deeper and staged knowledge would be good."

Three Steps Wiser - WcP Reading & Reflection Vol. 03

2008/09/02
WcP.Market.Watch

Browser wars: Google's Chrome takes on Microsoft

New contender in the browser wars: Google to launch open source web browser Chrome on Tuesday, takes on Microsoft

www.worldculturepictorial.com/ blog/ archive/ all/ 2008/09/02

Dean Goodluck

2008/09/03
WCP.Tomorrows.History

"I leave you free from both men" - Saint's last words in Year 366

03 Sep 301: Saint Marinus founded San Marino, one of the smallest nations and the world's oldest republic still in existence

www.worldculturepictorial.com/blog/archive/all/2008/09/03

Three Steps Wiser - WcP Reading & Reflection Vol. 03

2008/09/04
WcP.Dare.Say

*Dr. Ron Paul,
candidate in 2008 election,
once called "Young Lion"
and "Lion of Liberty", never yields*

Ron Paul addresses crowd of more than 10,000 people at Minneapolis rally, counter-convention rivals RNC next door

www.worldculturepictorial.com/blog/archive/all/2008/09/04

Dean Goodluck

2008/09/05
WCP.Story.Teller

The largest vessel ever sunk to make a reef: 44,000 tons, 888-foot long

Warship now a home for fish: U.S.S. Oriskany, The Great Carrier Reef, is largest vessel ever sunk to make a reef

www.worldculturepictorial.com/blog/archive/all/2008/09/05

Three Steps Wiser - WcP Reading & Reflection Vol. 03

2008/09/05
WcP.Watchful.Eye

Chunk of ice shelf size of Manhattan breaks away from Arctic

Irreversible loss: 4,500-year-old 19-square-mile ice shelf breaks away in Canada, 10x loss expected this summer

www.worldculturepictorial.com/blog/archive/all/2008/09/05

Dean Goodluck

2008/09/06
WCP.Scientific.Mind

Electric minivan?
Sounds attractive

Electric tank-car of the future?
The Hinterland 1 Concept Car - electric minivan with Prius-like aerodynamics

www.worldculturepictorial.com/blog/archive/all/2008/09/06

Reader Comments

(not in chronological order)
- 2016/05/30 - "The designers are not always working hand in hand with the engineers and sometimes at the beginning of a certain prototype, the exterior doesn't always match the interior. It is not only electric, but aerodynamic too."

- 2013/08/20 - "The exterior is ok, drag coefficient is ok, the whole idea is brilliant bar one thing - 28" wheels.. Why? What for? I don't get it.."
- 2009/05/25 - "Cool idea, very difficult to implement. The curved top looks *stunning* for a mini transporter. Thing is that it eliminates so much head and shoulder room that it's not going to happen as beautifully as this is drawn, unless the bottom is significantly wider than the top. As it's currently drawn, it'll seat three comfortably: One behind the other."
- 2013/03/25 - "GM has been testing electric versions of three of its cars in small trials in India, China, and South Korea, and will use what it learned there about driver preferences when it engineers the Spark EV. Hope we will have a better and planet safe car in near future."

Dean Goodluck

2008/09/07
WCP.Humor

Norwegian Sir with wings: knighted penguin Sir Nils Olav

World's most decorated penguin:
Sir Nils Olav, honorary colonel-in-chief
of Norwegian King's Guard, now a knight

www.worldculturepictorial.com/ blog/ archive/ all/ 2008/09/07

Three Steps Wiser - WcP Reading & Reflection Vol. 03

2008/09/07
WcP.Poetic.Thought

*A woman knows
the face of the man she loves
like a sailor knows the open sea.*

"A woman knows
the face of the man she loves
like a sailor knows the open sea."
- Honoré de Balzac

www.worldculturepictorial.com/blog/archive/all/2008/09/07

Dean Goodluck

2008/09/08
WCP.Movie.Critic

Fallen for WALL-E? More animation films reconnect with Nature

Animation films with message to reconnect with Nature - among 9 top animated enviro-flicks to watch, after Wall-E

www.worldculturepictorial.com/blog/archive/all/2008/09/08

Reader Comments

- 2014/12/14 - "This is a good list. Now I have something worthwhile and educational to watch with my kids."
- 2017/08/18 - "One could argue that what makes The Simpsons so side-achingly funny is not just the grand over-arching humor, but also the little things, the wisecracks, the peripheral gags."

Three Steps Wiser - WcP Reading & Reflection Vol. 03

2008/09/09
WcP.Observer

Roger Federer now just one win away from breaking Pete Sampras' record of 14 Grand Slam titles

Season turnaround: an emotional Federer claims 5th consecutive US Open victory, sets sights on Sampras' record

www.worldculturepictorial.com/ blog/ archive/ all/ 2008/ 09/ 09

Dean Goodluck

2008/09/10
WCP.Scientific.Mind

It's physics. Biggest and most complex machine on Earth, Large Hadron Collider fires first beam

Biggest physics experiment in history underway: Large Hadron Collider passes operational test, fires first beam

www.worldculturepictorial.com/blog/archive/all/2008/09/10

Three Steps Wiser - WcP Reading & Reflection Vol. 03

2008/09/11
WcP.Ambassador

*There was never a good war
or a bad peace.*

"There was never a good war
or a bad peace."
- Benjamin Franklin

www.worldculturepictorial.com/blog/archive/all/2008/09/11

Dean Goodluck

2008/09/12
WcP.Art

Fashion in a slimmer economy

At New York Fashion Week Spring-Summer 2009, designers bend fashions to fit a slimmer economy

www.worldculturepictorial.com/blog/archive/all/2008/09/12

Three Steps Wiser - WcP Reading & Reflection Vol. 03

2008/09/13
WcP.Humor

Animated show "The Simpsons" by Groening, airing on Fox network, longest-running comedy in prime time

"The Simpsons" wins 10th best cartoon Emmy Award - US television's highest honor for a prime-time cartoon

www.worldculturepictorial.com/blog/archive/all/2008/09/13

Dean Goodluck

2008/09/14
WCP.System.Thinker

"Perfect Flight": Air New Zealand cuts waiting time, trims flying time, saves 1,200 gallons of fuel

World first fuel-saving carbon-cutting program: Air New Zealand passengers take a ride on the "perfect flight"

www.worldculturepictorial.com/blog/archive/all/2008/09/14

Three Steps Wiser - WcP Reading & Reflection Vol. 03

2008/09/15
WcP.Poetic.Thought

Collective poetry book:
a solid year 1797-1798,
Wordsworth and Coleridge
had nothing but inspiration

15 Sep 1795. "Lyrical Ballads" published by Samuel Taylor Coleridge and William Wordsworth

www.worldculturepictorial.com/blog/archive/all/2008/09/15

Dean Goodluck

2008/09/16
WCP.Market.Watch

*Downward spiral:
158-year-old Lehman Brothers
filed largest bankruptcy;
Merrill Lynch sold*

Lehman bankrupt, Merrill sold;
worst day on Wall Street since 9/11 shakes
major markets worldwide, shares tumble

www.worldculturepictorial.com/blog/archive/all/2008/09/16

Reader Comments

♦ 2011/06/16 – "I really appreciate your post. It gives an outstanding idea that is very helpful for all the people on the web. Thanks for sharing this information and I'll love to read your next post too."

Three Steps Wiser - WcP Reading & Reflection Vol. 03

2008/09/17
WcP.Philosophy

History is a race between education and catastrophe.

"History is a race between education and catastrophe."
- H. G. Wells

www.worldculturepictorial.com/blog/archive/all/2008/09/17

Dean Goodluck

2008/09/18
WCP.Observer

Time for zero-emission car: all-electric luxury Tesla sedan on the way

All-electric car, 240+ miles per charge, 0 to 60 mph in under 6 seconds, to be built in San Jose Tesla factory

www.worldculturepictorial.com/ blog/ archive/ all/ 2008/09/18

Reader Comments

- 2012/06/19 – "I heard a lot of great things about Tesla Motors cars, a friend of mine bought one the last year and he loves it."

Three Steps Wiser - WcP Reading & Reflection Vol. 03

- 2012/08/13 - "More and more car makers are going for electric cars. I'm still in doubt as to the effectiveness of electric cars. I know they have their benefits but a lot of downsides too. Yes, their parts can be readily available but are the charging stations enough? I heard they can't even travel in long distances and takes a while to charge."
- 2012/11/02 - "They build their charging stations in all states and most big cities. So you won't feel lack of attention to your car. As for me, next year I'm going to replace my old 2005 Chevy Charger with a new Tesla Model S. I can't wait to see it saving my money for fuel."
- 2017/08/18 - "All of the cars shown above are so good and I really loved to drive them from my home. But only suitable for people who do good maintenance of them."
- 2017/10/31 - "It is very good design car, but how with top speed?"
- 2017/11/25 - "It's a very useful article. Nowadays the era is the electric car era so, everyone wants to buy hybrid cars. But these prices are very high, slowly it will be cheap, easy to buy."

Dean Goodluck

2008/09/19
wcp.life.Coach

"Do I really want that CT scan?"
A chest CT scan is equivalent to about 100 X-rays

"Do I really want that CT scan?" Study shows increased radiation exposure, cancer risks, tests often unnecessary

www.worldculturepictorial.com/blog/archive/all/2008/09/19

Reader Comments

(not in chronological order)
- 2016/12/15 – "The technology is increasing day by day in medical field at the same time the side effects like radiation are also increasing. These companies who manufacture the medical scanning machines use electromagnetic wave to detect the problem in our body. Those waves create radiation and cause others problems to patients in their body."

Three Steps Wiser - WcP Reading & Reflection Vol. 03

- 2013/11/15 - "A lot of doctors are using CT scans for lung cancer screenings and blood vessel inspections, however the patients are advised to make a CT scan and take such dose of radiation only once an year. My niece is involved in the incentaHEALTH program, she is traveling a lot and tries to stay away from the scans at the airports. There are a lot of studies about the effects of computer tomography scans and unfortunately a lot of doctors won't admit that CT scans are harmful because they have become a potential source of income."
- 2012/04/10 - "'... CT scans have become the primary driver of the nation's rising radiation exposure.' I think we are to blame for that! You don't need to take a CT scan for every little niggle."
- 2016/12/07 - "nice research"
- 2016/12/08 - "I read in some article online that people working in medical laboratories have more chances for getting cancer. It is due to the frequent exposure to radiations. It is better not to conduct scans on you until you think something is seriously wrong."

- 2016/12/02 - "These are some really significant information about CT scans. We have heard about the radiation exposure we are getting when subjected to such scans. This post clearly describes the health issues that could be faced due to the exposure of radiation."
- 2016/04/07 - "This is the website that has helped me to know more on the global culture. The posts that are shared here on the site are so interesting and informative. Keep on sharing more and more posts like this."
- 2016/11/17 - "It is shocking to hear about the health issues related to undergoing a CT scan. The two infographics clearly demonstrate the working of these medical technologies and also their possible health risks associated with high doses of radiation which is typical of a CT scan."
- 2016/10/18 - "You have shared a very informative blog about the advantages and disadvantages of CT scan. It helped me a lot to understand about the harmful effects of CT scan. The radiations are very harmful to our body. There will be the risk of cancer."
- 2016/10/06 - "I like your post. You have done really good work. I appreciate your working style at the end just my request is please share with us some more great post..."

Three Steps Wiser - WcP Reading & Reflection Vol. 03

- 2016/06/15 - "Many of us are confused about this CT scan and this article really helped a lot in making decisions. There are lot of things explained here in this wonderful piece of writing about the CT scan and I am really thankful to the blog for this."
- 2016/06/07 - "I too have such doubts on CT scan and here in this article it is clearly explained about the matters on CT scan. I am really satisfied after reading this article and I would like to thank the blog for sharing such wonderful piece of writing."
- 2016/10/18 - "Great job for publishing such a beneficial web site. Your web log isn't only useful but it is additionally really creative too. There tend to be not many people who can certainly write not so simple posts that artistically. Continue the nice writing"
- 2016/10/09 - "I am for the first time here. I found this board and finding It truly helpful and it helped me out a lot. I hope to present something back and help others such as you helped me."

Dean Goodluck

2008/09/20
WCP.Art

Southern Hemisphere Paris? "Foodie" often heard in Melbourne

Taking best of international cuisine, Melbourne becomes world's latest destination for inventive, delicious food

www.worldculturepictorial.com/blog/archive/all/2008/09/20

Reader Comments

- 2010/04/29 - "Melbourne may be oft-overlooked when it comes to paying respect to the world's culinary capitals. Sydney usually steals the culinary thunder in Australia, but Oz's scrappy second city is not always outdone. There are numerous standout restaurants that have helped shaped Melbourne's burgeoning reputation as a food destination. After the jump, a list of a few Melbourne eateries where you truly can't go wrong."

Three Steps Wiser - WcP Reading & Reflection Vol. 03

2008/09/21
WcP.Poetic.Thought

Romance like a ghost escapes touching; it is always where you are not, not where you are...

"Romance like a ghost escapes touching; it is always where you are not, not where you are. The interview or conversation was prose at the time, but it is poetry in the memory."
- George William Curtis

www.worldculturepictorial.com/blog/archive/all/2008/09/21

Dean Goodluck

2008/09/22
WcP.Observer

Tony Blair's point of view at Yale

Tony Blair begins Faith and Globalization lecture series at Yale, says religion has potential to harm or heal

www.worldculturepictorial.com/blog/archive/all/2008/09/22

Three Steps Wiser - WcP Reading & Reflection Vol. 03

2008/09/23
WcP.Scientific.Mind

Large Hadron Collider,
the most powerful atom smasher,
switched on two weeks ago,
now hibernates

Large Hadron Collider hibernates after wrong sort of big bang caused by hellion leak, to re-awaken in Spring'09

www.worldculturepictorial.com/blog/archive/all/2008/09/23

Dean Goodluck

2008/09/24
WCP.Philosophy

Earth provides enough to satisfy every man's need, but not every man's greed.

"**E**arth provides enough to satisfy every man's need, but not every man's greed."
- Mahatma Gandhi

www.worldculturepictorial.com/blog/archive/all/2008/09/24

Three Steps Wiser - WcP Reading & Reflection Vol. 03

2008/09/25
WcP.Market.Watch

*Stock market's wild swings -
rich gets richer,
and someone gets poorer*

Main St wonders "people responsible for this are making half a million a year, why do we have to bail them out?"

www.worldculturepictorial.com/ blog/ archive/ all/ 2008/ 09/ 25

Dean Goodluck

2008/09/26
WCP.Scientific.Mind

*First spacewalk:
three decades of hoping,
ten years of training*

Countdown begins for China's first spacewalk: Shenzhou-7 spaceship launches into orbit with 3 Chinese astronauts

www.worldculturepictorial.com/blog/archive/all/2008/09/26

Three Steps Wiser - WcP Reading & Reflection Vol. 03

2008/09/27
WcP.Story.Teller

Fusionman
"flies a little bit like a bird"
with homemade
rocket-powered wing

Historical flight - Swiss "Rocketman" Yves Rossy crosses English Channel with homemade jet wing in 10 minutes

www.worldculturepictorial.com/blog/archive/all/2008/09/27

Dean Goodluck

2008/09/28
WCP.Movie.Critic

*Paul Newman,
a consummate charmer,
dedicated himself to his cause,
racing cars, wife and family*

"A star you could look up to both on and off the screen": Hollywood legend, philanthropist Paul Newman 1925-2008

www.worldculturepictorial.com/blog/archive/all/2008/09/28

Three Steps Wiser - WcP Reading & Reflection Vol. 03

2008/09/29
WcP.Scientific.Mind

*3 technology powers
US, Russia, now China,
have their astronauts walk in space*

World's most exclusive club:
Russia, US, now China have technology to
allow their astronauts to walk in space

www.worldculturepictorial.com/blog/archive/all/2008/09/29

Dean Goodluck

2008/09/30
WcP.Movie.Critic

Hometown. They sing, rehearse, perform, and they are in their eighties

Feel young at heart? In your 30s,40s...? They sure do in their 80s,90s, singing and performing: Young@Heart Chorus

www.worldculturepictorial.com/blog/archive/all/2008/09/30

Three Steps Wiser - WcP Reading & Reflection Vol. 03

2008/09/30
WcP.Poetic.Thought

Poem
"Blow, blow, thou winter wind
Thou art not so unkind
As man's ingratitude"
- William Shakespeare

Blow, blow, thou winter wind
Thou art not so unkind
As man's ingratitude;
Thy tooth is not so keen,
Because thou art not seen,
Although thy breath be rude.

Heigh-ho! sing, heigh-ho!
　　unto the green holly:
Most friendship is feigning,
　　most loving mere folly:
Then heigh-ho, the holly!
This life is most jolly.

www.worldculturepictorial.com/blog/archive/all/2008/09/30

Dean Goodluck

2008/09/30
WCP.Poetic.Thought

Poem
"Freeze, freeze thou bitter sky,
That does not bite so nigh
As benefits forgot"
- William Shakespeare

Freeze, freeze thou bitter sky,
That does not bite so nigh
As benefits forgot:
Though thou the waters warp,
Thy sting is not so sharp
As a friend remembered not.
Heigh-ho! sing, heigh-ho!
    unto the green holly:
Most friendship is feigning,
    most loving mere folly:
Then heigh-ho, the holly!
This life is most jolly.

- Blow, Blow, Thou Winter Wind
by William Shakespeare

www.worldculturepictorial.com/blog/archive/all/2008/09/30

Three Steps Wiser - WcP Reading & Reflection Vol. 03

2008/10/01
WcP.Dare.Say

3rd most popular in the race in most opinion polls: 2008

Independent US presidential candidate Nader and running mate Gonzalez banned from debates, on ballot in 45 states

www.worldculturepictorial.com/blog/archive/all/2008/10/01

Dean Goodluck

2008/10/02
WCP.Common.Sense

Math.
$700 billion to bail out
drained $635 billion

Unforeseen consequences - 2002 vote for Iraq War dug $635-billion hole in 6 years, now another vote for $700 billion to fill it?

www.worldculturepictorial.com/blog/archive/all/2008/10/02

2008/10/03
WcP.Scientific.Mind

Queen Elizabeth II's vision to reign over the wind

Queen Elizabeth II buys world largest wind turbine - towers over Big Ben, to light up thousands of British homes

www.worldculturepictorial.com/ blog/ archive/ all/ 2008/ 10/ 03

Reader Comments

(not in chronological order)
- 2012/04/21 - "No wonder years from now, Queen Elizabeth II will rule the wind turbine industry. Her wealth can surely afford the costs of wind turbines. Britain is lucky enough to have her."
- 2012/08/29 - "That's so true. She's indeed a tough old lady!"

- 2012/11/27 - "Excellent post and wonderful blog, I really like this type of interesting articles keep it up. I am really loving the theme/design of your web site."
- 2012/03/20 - "Hi... Very true. Good article and good comments."
- 2013/04/02 - "It is really surprising news that Queen Elizabeth II buys the largest wind turbine. News has revealed to Fortune that Her windmill has been super-sized to ten megawatts, producing five times the power generated by typical big turbines currently in commercial operation. Glad to know this information."
- 2012/02/09 - "The Queen's turbine prototype will be the flagship for Clipper's Britannia Project, an effort to create a new generation of massive-megawatt turbines to be placed on deep-sea floating platforms."
- 2011/10/17 - "Wow! Queen Elizabeth II has bought the world's biggest wind turbine which can be used to light up thousands of British homes. I think there will be some people who may use commercial lighting suppliers to install light systems in their homes."

Three Steps Wiser - WeP Reading & Reflection Vol. 03

- 2013/01/25 - "You make it entertaining and you even now manage to help keep it wise. I cant wait to go through additional from you. That is really an incredible weblog."
- 2013/01/28 - "Brilliant safe internet for my child that will grant the incentive and foundation for my work. I wonder if I can state the article as a reference in my work. Thanks!"
- 2011/09/18 - "Wind turbines are just one of the ways to harness nature's power to generate energy. If possible, the Queen can also look into tidal energy. The are machines that harness the powerful force of waves and convert them into energy. Though they might not be as efficient as wind energy now, with a bit of investment from the Queen, I bet it could be the wave of the future, pun not intended."
- 2011/07/26 - "You have innocent information about electricity projects. I liked it. Thanks for your information and for taking the time to put up the photos and imparting your words of wisdom - we all enjoy it."
- 2010/05/22 - "Wind turbines are used to generate electricity from the kinetic power of the wind. Historically they were more frequently used as a mechanical device to turn machinery."

Dean Goodluck

2008/10/04
WcP.Observer

*EV show in Paris.
Two years ago,
electric cars impossible*

Revival of the electric car: against industry's gloomy forecast, hybrid and electric cars light up Paris Auto Show

www.worldculturepictorial.com/blog/archive/all/2008/10/04

Reader Comments

(not in chronological order)

♦ 2012/08/13 – "Whoa! These are some cool electric cars. Of those featured, the Nissan Nuvu is very different. Its interior and exterior are unique compared to other Nissan cars. It's very cute! I would love to test drive one."

- 2012/12/29 - "I think that if the electric cars will have success we can expect that many of us will get rid of their cars. There are several car donation agencies and I think I would like to buy a new car. I'm very happy for you, also!"
- 2016/06/08 - "It's absolutely INSANE to know how far cars have come over the span of 8 years. Back in 2008, electric cars were something of the future. These days, they're faster and much more efficient than gasoline vehicles. It's amazing to know how many improvements can be made in less than a decade. Then again, technology is always advancing forwards. Whether in the automotive industry or the technological industry. And that's far from the tip of the iceburg - there's been heavy advancements in mobile technology as well. Technology is an amazing thing.. I cannot wait to see where we'll be 10 years from now!"
- 2011/06/01 - "Good thing you've posted this one sir. I will be using some information of yours for my thesis. Thanks!"

- 2012/06/25 - "Electric motors are really very innovative.. these motorcars stand for fuel efficiency which comes with reduction of air and sound pollution. Electric cars are true example of Eco friendly vehicles."
- 2012/07/04 - "The presence of electrical cars in the market today is truly beneficial to the public since it merely addresses the problem with the skyrocketing price of gas. On the other hand, the purpose of these vehicles is truly Eco-friendly and the Paris auto show was made to let people know about it. Not just car models are being show here however because there are also maintenance process that's going to help people in times of car troubles. Plus the fact that they also revealed efficient stuff truly meant for replacement and tuning which includes the basic such as front bumper cover, ignition system, transmission etc."

Three Steps Wiser - WcP Reading & Reflection Vol. 03

2008/10/05
WcP.Story.Teller

*Brazilian coastguards'
air force plane offers
lost young penguins
a free ride*

Homeless: lost penguins stranded on Brazilian beaches get lift home from air force

www.worldculturepictorial.com/blog/archive/all/2008/10/05

Dean Goodluck

www.worldculturepictorial.com/blog/archive/all/2008/10/06

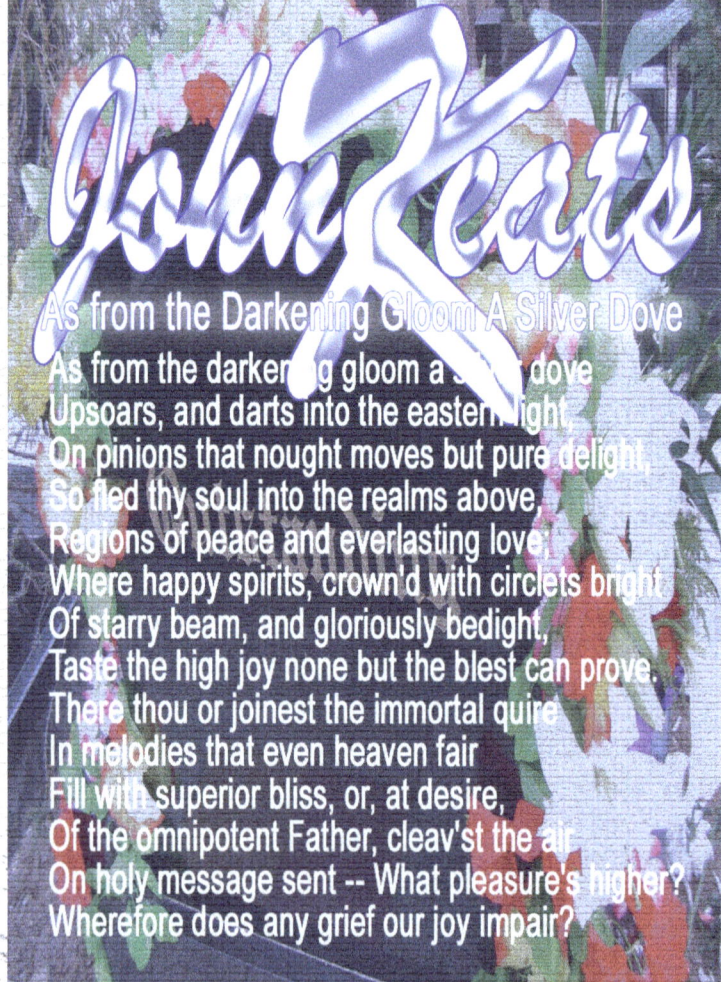

John Keats

As from the Darkening Gloom A Silver Dove

As from the darkening gloom a silver dove
Upsoars, and darts into the eastern light,
On pinions that nought moves but pure delight,
So fled thy soul into the realms above,
Regions of peace and everlasting love;
Where happy spirits, crown'd with circlets bright
Of starry beam, and gloriously bedight,
Taste the high joy none but the blest can prove.
There thou or joinest the immortal quire
In melodies that even heaven fair
Fill with superior bliss, or, at desire,
Of the omnipotent Father, cleav'st the air
On holy message sent -- What pleasure's higher?
Wherefore does any grief our joy impair?

2008/10/06
WcP.Poetic.Thought

Poem in Art
"So fled thy soul into the realms above, / Regions of peace and everlasting love"
- John Keats

As from the darkening gloom a silver dove
Upsoars, and darts into the eastern light,
On pinions that nought moves
    but pure delight,
So fled thy soul into the realms above,
Regions of peace and everlasting love;
Where happy spirits, crown'd
    with circlets bright
Of starry beam, and gloriously bedight,
Taste the high joy none
    but the blest can prove.
There thou or joinest the immortal quire
In melodies that even heaven fair
Fill with superior bliss, or, at desire,
Of the omnipotent Father, cleav'st the air
On holy message sent --
    What pleasure's higher?
Wherefore does any grief our joy impair?

- John Keats

Dean Goodluck

2008/10/06
WcP.Art

Luckiest photographer met Einstein, Churchill, Picasso, and Hemingway

Work of legendary portraitist Yousuf Karsh celebrated at Boston exhibit - Churchill, Hepburn, Picasso, and more

www.worldculturepictorial.com/blog/archive/all/2008/10/06

Three Steps Wiser - WcP Reading & Reflection Vol. 03

2008/10/07
WcP.System.Thinker

5,487 mammals on Earth: 76 gone, 1,141 in danger of extinction

Getting worse: half of mammals in decline, 1 in 4 faces extinction; conservation can bring species back

www.worldculturepictorial.com/blog/archive/all/2008/10/07

Dean Goodluck

2008/10/08
WCP.WatchfulEye

*How big is 10 trillion?
Its digits beat
National Debt Clock
in New York*

Trillion? US national debt clock in Times Square runs out of digits for the first time as debt exceeds $10 trillion

www.worldculturepictorial.com/blog/archive/all/2008/10/08

Three Steps Wiser - WcP Reading & Reflection Vol. 03

2008/10/09
WcP.Story.Teller

1783, birth of hot air balloons carrying human passengers

37th Annual Albuquerque International Balloon Fiesta marks 225th anniversary of first manned balloon flight

www.worldculturepictorial.com/blog/archive/all/2008/10/09

Dean Goodluck

2008/10/10
WCP.Common.Sense

*It is a thousand times better
to have common sense
without education than...*

"It is a thousand times better
to have common sense without education
than
to have education without common sense."
- Robert Green Ingersoll

www.worldculturepictorial.com/blog/archive/all/2008/10/10

- 2016/11/28 – "Thank you."
- 2017/02/22 – "Sensible answer. Most of the students don't have their own sense. Education make a person sensible to get best lifestyle. Students can get education for betterment in future."

Three Steps Wiser - WeP Reading & Reflection Vol. 03

- 2017/07/14 - "It is said that common sense is not common and it is really true. Common sense is very important for everything. In this blog we would read that if common sense is important or education is more important and how both are important for us."
- 2017/07/17 - "Hi there nice post. Education plays a vital role in our daily life. Without education, we can not do anything."
- 2017/12/13 - "Online Education System - The growth and rise of internet has made it possible for students to enroll and study at best online universities and thus making it easier for literally anyone to shape their career in the way they want to and at any time in their career."

Dean Goodluck

2008/10/11
WCP.Scientific.Mind

Night is not what it was - how do you feel with light everywhere?

Turning out the lights - light pollution squanders energy, raises cancer risks, disturbs wildlife and ecosystem

www.worldculturepictorial.com/blog/archive/all/2008/10/11

Reader Comments

♦ 2010/05/24 - "Landscape lighting doesn't have to cost a fortune anymore and there are a few things you can do to ensure you get the best possible price."

♦ 2008/10/11 - "Love your pictures.
Excellent blog, I found you through Google alerts because this is a subject near and dear to me.
I am a member of International Dark Sky Association and encourage anyone interested in recovering our night skies (the stars are there, we just can't see them!) to give what you can to IDA or your local chapter and purchase only dark sky compliant lights.
Cheryl"

Dean Goodluck

2008/10/12
WcP.Story.Teller

1492. Columbus wrote in his journal, "as I saw that they (local natives) were very friendly to us"

12 Oct 1492: Christopher Columbus lands in the Bahamas, believes he has reached East Asia

www.worldculturepictorial.com/blog/archive/all/2008/10/12

2008/10/12
WcP.Humor

Shall I crack any of those old jokes, master, at which the audience never fail to laugh?

"Shall I crack any of those old jokes, master, at which the audience never fail to laugh?"
- Aristophanes, "The Frogs", 405 B.C.
Greek Athenian comic dramatist
www.worldculturepictorial.com/blog/archive/all/2008/10/12

Robert Louis Stevenson

"Wine is bottled poetry."

Let's toast

Leisure reading along the journey of publishing this book

Dean Goodluck

Lord Byron

'Tis Ode to Napoleon Buonoparte

I

'TIS done -- but yesterday a King!
   And arm'd with Kings to strive --
And now thou art a nameless thing:
   So abject -- yet alive!
Is this the man of thousand thrones,
Who strew'd our earth with hostile bones,
   And can he thus survive?
Since he, miscall'd the Morning Star,
Nor man nor fiend hath fallen so far.

II

Ill-minded man! why scourge thy kind
   Who bow'd so low the knee?
By gazing on thyself grown blind,
   Thou taught'st the rest to see.
With might unquestion'd, -- power to save, --
Thine only gift hath been the grave,
   To those that worshipp'd thee;
   Nor till thy fall could mortals guess
Ambition's less than littleness!

Three Steps Wiser - WcP Reading & Reflection Vol. 03

Poem in Art
"yesterday a King! / now thou art a nameless thing...Ambition's less than littleness!"

Lord Byron

I.
Tis done--but yesterday a King!
And arm'd with Kings to strive--
And now thou art a nameless thing:
So abject--yet alive!
Is this the man of thousand thrones,
Who strew'd our earth with hostile bones,
And can he thus survive?
Since he, miscall'd the Morning Star,
Nor man nor fiend hath fallen so far.

II.
Ill-minded man! why scourge thy kind
Who bow'd so low the knee?
By gazing on thyself grown blind,
Thou taught'st the rest to see.
With might unquestion'd--power to save,--
Thine only gift hath been the grave
To those that worshipp'd thee;
Nor till thy fall could mortals guess
Ambition's less than littleness!

- from Ode To Napoleon Buonaparte
by Lord Byron

Dean Goodluck

A Broken Friendship

Poem
A Broken Friendship
Samuel Taylor Coleridge

Alas! they had been friends in youth;
But whispering tongues can poison truth;
And constancy lives in realms above;
And life is thorny; and youth is vain;
And to be wroth with one we love,
Doth work like madness in the brain.
And thus is chanced, as I divine,
With Roland and Sir Leoline.
Each spake words of high disdain
And insult to his heart's best brother:
They parted - ne'er to meet again!
But never either found another
To free the hollow heart from painting -
They stood aloof, the scars remaining,
Like cliffs which had been rent asunder;
A dreary see now flows between; -
But neither heat, nor frost, nor thunder
Shall wholly do away, I ween,
The marks of that which once hath been

- A Broken Friendship
by Samuel Taylor Coleridge

Dean Goodluck

Emily Dickinson

"Nature" is what we see—
The Hill—the Afternoon—
Squirrel—Eclipse— the Bumble bee—
Nay—Nature is Heaven—
Nature is what we hear—
The Bobolink—the Sea—
Thunder—the Cricket—
Nay—Nature is Harmony—
Nature is what we know—
Yet have no art to say—
So impotent Our Wisdom is
To her Simplicity.

Three Steps Wiser - WcP Reading & Reflection Vol. 03

Poem in Art
"Nature" Is What We See
Emily Dickinson

"Nature" is what we see—
The Hill—the Afternoon—
Squirrel—Eclipse— the Bumble bee—
Nay—Nature is Heaven—
Nature is what we hear—
The Bobolink—the Sea—
Thunder—the Cricket—
Nay—Nature is Harmony—
Nature is what we know—
Yet have no art to say—
So impotent Our Wisdom is
To her Simplicity.

- "Nature" Is What We See
by Emily Dickinson

Dean Goodluck

Rupert Brooke

The Beginning

Some day I shall rise and leave my friends
And seek you again through the world's far ends,
You whom I found so fair
(Touch of your hands and smell of your hair!),
My only god in the days that were.
My eager feet shall find you again,
Though the sullen years and the mark of pain
Have changed you wholly; for I shall know
(How could I forget having loved you so?),
In the sad half-light of evening,
The face that was all my sunrising.
So then at the ends of the earth I'll stand
And hold you fiercely be either hand,
And seeing your age and ashen hair
I'll curse the thing that once you were,
Because it is changed and pale and old
(Lips that were scarlet, hair that was gold!),
And I loved you before you were old and wise,
When the flame of youth was strong in your eyes,
—And my heart is sick with memories.

Three Steps Wiser - WcP Reading & Reflection Vol. 03

Poem in Art
The Beginning
Rupert Brooke

Some day I shall rise and leave my friends
And seek you again through the world's far ends,
You whom I found so fair
(Touch of your hands and smell of your hair!),
My only god in the days that were.
My eager feet shall find you again,
Though the sullen years and the mark of pain
Have changed you wholly; for I shall know
(How could I forget having loved you so?),
In the sad half-light of evening,
The face that was all my sunrising.
So then at the ends of the earth I'll stand
And hold you fiercely by either hand,
And seeing your age and ashen hair
I'll curse the thing that once you were,
Because it is changed and pale and old
(Lips that were scarlet, hair that was gold!),
And I loved you before you were old and wise,
When the flame of youth was strong in your eyes,
-- And my heart is sick with memories.

- The Beginning
by Rupert Brooke

Dean Goodluck

the Sailor Boy

Poem
The Sailor-Boy
John Clare

Tis three years and a quarter
    since I left my own fireside
To go aboard a ship through love,
    and plough the ocean wide.
I crossed my native fields,
    where the scarlet poppies grew,
And the groundlark left his nest
    like a neighbour which I knew.

The pigeons from the dove cote
    cooed over the old lane,
The crow flocks from the oakwood
    went flopping oer the grain;
Like lots of dear old neighbours
    whom I shall see no more
They greeted me that morning
    I left the English shore.

Dean Goodluck

The sun was just a-rising
    above the heath of furze,
And the shadows grow to giants;
    that bright ball never stirs:
There the shepherds lay
    with their dogs by their side,
And they started up and barked
    as my shadow they espied.

A maid of early morning
    twirled her mop upon the moor;
I wished her my farewell
    before she closed the door.
My friends I left behind me
    for other places new,
Crows and pigeons all were strangers
    as oer my head they flew.

Trees and bushes were all strangers,
    the hedges and the lanes,
The steeples and the houses
    and broad untrodden plains.
I passed the pretty milkmaid
    with her red and rosy face;
I knew not where I met her,
    I was strange to the place.

At last I saw the ocean,
    a pleasing sight to me:
I stood upon the shore of
    a mighty glorious sea.
The waves in easy motion
    went rolling on their way,
English colours were a-flying
    where the British squadron lay.

I left my honest parents,
    the church clock and the village;
I left the lads and lasses,
    the labour and the tillage;
To plough the briny ocean,
    which soon became my joy--
I sat and sang among the shrouds,
    a lonely sailor-boy.

- The Sailor-Boy
by John Clare

Dean Goodluck

Paradise Lost

Poem
Paradise Lost: Book 01
(lines 392-543)
John Milton

First, Moloch, horrid king, besmeared with blood
Of human sacrifice, and parents' tears;
Though, for the noise of drums and timbrels loud,
Their children's cries unheard that
    passed through fire
To his grim idol. Him the Ammonite
Worshiped in Rabba and her watery plain,
In Argob and in Basan, to the stream
Of utmost Arnon. Nor content with such
Audacious neighbourhood, the wisest heart
Of Solomon he led by fraud to build
His temple right against the temple of God
On that opprobrious hill, and made his grove
The pleasant valley of Hinnom, Tophet thence
And black Gehenna called, the type of Hell.
Next Chemos, th' obscene dread of Moab's sons,
From Aroar to Nebo and the wild
Of southmost Abarim; in Hesebon
And Horonaim, Seon's realm, beyond
The flowery dale of Sibma clad with vines,
And Eleale to th' Asphaltic Pool:

Dean Goodluck

Peor his other name, when he enticed
Israel in Sittim, on their march from Nile,
To do him wanton rites, which cost them woe.
Yet thence his lustful orgies he enlarged
Even to that hill of scandal, by the grove
Of Moloch homicide, lust hard by hate,
Till good Josiah drove them thence to Hell.
With these came they who, from the bordering flood
Of old Euphrates to the brook that parts
Egypt from Syrian ground, had general names
Of Baalim and Ashtaroth--those male,
These feminine. For Spirits, when they please,
Can either sex assume, or both; so soft
And uncompounded is their essence pure,
Not tried or manacled with joint or limb,
Nor founded on the brittle strength of bones,
Like cumbrous flesh; but, in what shape they choose,
Dilated or condensed, bright or obscure,
Can execute their airy purposes,
And works of love or enmity fulfil.
For those the race of Israel oft forsook
Their Living Strength, and unfrequented left
His righteous altar, bowing lowly down

To bestial gods; for which their heads as low
Bowed down in battle, sunk before the spear
Of despicable foes. With these in troop
Came Astoreth, whom the Phoenicians called
Astarte, queen of heaven, with crescent horns;
To whose bright image nightly by the moon
Sidonian virgins paid their vows and songs;
In Sion also not unsung, where stood
Her temple on th' offensive mountain, built
By that uxorious king whose heart, though large,
Beguiled by fair idolatresses, fell
To idols foul. Thammuz came next behind,
Whose annual wound in Lebanon allured
The Syrian damsels to lament his fate
In amorous ditties all a summer's day,
While smooth Adonis from his native rock
Ran purple to the sea, supposed with blood
Of Thammuz yearly wounded: the love-tale
Infected Sion's daughters with like heat,
Whose wanton passions in the sacred proch
Ezekiel saw, when, by the vision led,
His eye surveyed the dark idolatries
Of alienated Judah. Next came one

Dean Goodluck

Who mourned in earnest, when the captive ark
Maimed his brute image, head and hands lopt off,
In his own temple, on the grunsel-edge,
Where he fell flat and shamed his worshippers:
Dagon his name, sea-monster, upward man
And downward fish; yet had his temple high
Reared in Azotus, dreaded through the coast
Of Palestine, in Gath and Ascalon,
And Accaron and Gaza's frontier bounds.
Him followed Rimmon, whose delightful seat
Was fair Damascus, on the fertile banks
Of Abbana and Pharphar, lucid streams.
He also against the house of God was bold:
A leper once he lost, and gained a king--
Ahaz, his sottish conqueror, whom he drew
God's altar to disparage and displace
For one of Syrian mode, whereon to burn
His odious offerings, and adore the gods
Whom he had vanquished. After these appeared
A crew who, under names of old renown--
Osiris, Isis, Orus, and their train--
With monstrous shapes and sorceries abused
Fanatic Egypt and her priests to seek

Their wandering gods disguised in brutish forms
Rather than human. Nor did Israel scape
Th' infection, when their borrowed gold composed
The calf in Oreb; and the rebel king
Doubled that sin in Bethel and in Dan,
Likening his Maker to the grazed ox--
Jehovah, who, in one night, when he passed
From Egypt marching, equalled with one stroke
Both her first-born and all her bleating gods.
Belial came last; than whom a Spirit more lewd
Fell not from Heaven, or more gross to love
Vice for itself. To him no temple stood
Or altar smoked; yet who more oft than he
In temples and at altars, when the priest
Turns atheist, as did Eli's sons, who filled
With lust and violence the house of God?
In courts and palaces he also reigns,
And in luxurious cities, where the noise
Of riot ascends above their loftiest towers,
And injury and outrage; and, when night
Darkens the streets, then wander forth the sons
Of Belial, flown with insolence and wine.

Dean Goodluck

Witness the streets of Sodom, and that night
In Gibeah, when the hospitable door
Exposed a matron, to avoid worse rape.
These were the prime in order and in might:
The rest were long to tell; though far renowned
Th' Ionian gods--of Javan's issue held
Gods, yet confessed later than Heaven and Earth,
Their boasted parents;--Titan, Heaven's first-born,
With his enormous brood, and birthright seized
By younger Saturn: he from mightier Jove,
His own and Rhea's son, like measure found;
So Jove usurping reigned. These, first in Crete
And Ida known, thence on the snowy top
Of cold Olympus ruled the middle air,
Their highest heaven; or on the Delphian cliff,
Or in Dodona, and through all the bounds
Of Doric land; or who with Saturn old
Fled over Adria to th' Hesperian fields,
And o'er the Celtic roamed the utmost Isles.
All these and more came flocking; but with looks
Downcast and damp; yet such wherein appeared
Obscure some glimpse of joy
    to have found their Chief

Three Steps Wiser - WcP Reading & Reflection Vol. 03

Not in despair, to have found themselves not lost
In loss itself; which on his countenance cast
Like doubtful hue. But he, his wonted pride
Soon recollecting, with high words, that bore
Semblance of worth, not substance, gently raised
Their fainting courage, and dispelled their fears.
Then straight commands that, at the warlike sound
Of trumpets loud and clarions, be upreared
His mighty standard. That proud honour claimed
Azazel as his right, a Cherub tall:
Who forthwith from the glittering staff unfurled
Th' imperial ensign; which, full high advanced,
Shone like a meteor streaming to the wind,
With gems and golden lustre rich emblazed,
Seraphic arms and trophies; all the while
Sonorous metal blowing martial sounds:
At which the universal host up-sent
A shout that tore Hell's concave, and beyond
Frighted the reign of Chaos and old Night.

- from Paradise Lost: Book 01 (lines 392-543)
by John Milton

Dean Goodluck

Character

Three Steps Wiser - WcP Reading & Reflection Vol. 03

Poem in Art
A Character
William Wordsworth

I marvel how Nature could ever find space
For so many strange contrasts in one human face:
There's thought and no thought,
    and there's paleness and bloom
And bustle and sluggishness, pleasure and gloom.

There's weakness, and strength
    both redundant and vain;
Such strength as, if ever affliction and pain
Could pierce through a temper that's soft to disease,
Would be rational peace, a philosopher's ease.

There's indifference, alike when he fails or succeeds,
And attention full ten times as much
    as there needs;
Pride where there's no envy, there's so much of joy;
And mildness, and spirit both forward and coy.

Dean Goodluck

And I
for five centuries
right gladly would be
Such an odd
such a kind happy
creature as he.

~ William Wordsworth

There's freedom, and sometimes a diffident stare
Of shame scarcely seeming to know
    that she's there,
There's virtue, the title it surely may claim,
Yet wants heaven knows what to be
    worthy the name.

This picture from nature may seem to depart,
Yet the Man would at once run away
    with your heart;
And I for five centuries right gladly would be
Such an odd such a kind happy creature as he.

- A Character
by William Wordsworth

Publisher's Blog:
WcP Blog | World Culture Pictorial
www.worldculturepictorial.com

"The method for composing is phenomenal
furthermore the substance is first class
A debt of gratitude is in order for
that knowledge you give the perusers!"
- Anonymous

"Your site is valuable.
Appreciative for sharing!
Awe inspiring Blog!"
- Anonymous

"I always take pleasure in your articles.
You have a gift for discussing such
stirring topics in ingenious yet amusing ways.
Your posts help us realize that our troubles are
typical, and we can solve them in
ready to lend a hand ways..." - Angela

Dean Goodluck

Other Volumes in this Series

full color print
through and through
including art images

www.worldculturepictorial.com/one-step-wiser.html

Three Steps Wiser - WcP Reading & Reflection Vol. 03

Other Volumes in this Series

full color print
through and through
including art images

www.worldculturepictorial.com/one-step-wiser.html

Dean Goodluck

Other Volumes in this Series

b&w interior print
on classic creme paper
including art images

www.worldculturepictorial.com/one-step-wiser.html

Three Steps Wiser - WcP Reading & Reflection Vol. 03

www.ingramcontent.com/pod-product-compliance
Lightning Source LLC
Chambersburg PA
CBHW041324110526
44592CB00021B/2813